HMH |  **into Math**™

Getting Ready for High-Stakes Assessment

Grade 2

Contents

About *Getting Ready for High-Stakes Assessment* v

Assessment Item Types vi

Standards Practice

    Use Addition and Subtraction to Solve One- and Two-Step Problems 1

    Fluently Add and Subtract Within 20 Using Mental Strategies 3

    Determine Whether a Group has an Odd or Even Number of Members 5

    Use Addition to Find the Total Number in a Rectangular Array 7

    Understand that 100 can be Thought of as a Bundle of Ten Tens 9

    Understand that Some Numbers Refer to a Certain Number of Hundreds 11

    Count Within 1,000; Skip-Count by 5s, 10s, and 100s 13

    Read and Write Numbers to 1,000 15

    Compare Two Three-Digit Numbers 17

    Fluently Add and Subtract Within 100 19

    Add up to Four Two-Digit Numbers 21

    Add and Subtract Within 1,000 23

    Mentally Add or Subtract 10 or 100 to or From a Given Number 25

    Explain why Addition and Subtraction Strategies Work 27

    Measure the Length of an Object 29

    Describe the Relationship Between the Size of a Unit and Number of Units 31

    Estimate Lengths 33

    Measure to Determine How Much Longer one Object is than Another 35

    Use Addition and Subtraction to Solve Word Problems Involving Lengths 37

© Houghton Mifflin Harcourt Publishing Company

Represent Sums and Differences on a Number Line Diagram **39**

Tell and Write Time to the Nearest Five Minutes **41**

Solve Word Problems Involving Dollar Bills or Coins **43**

Generate Measurement Data and Show the Data on a Line Plot **45**

Draw a Picture Graph and a Bar Graph to Represent a Data Set **47**

Recognize and Draw Shapes Having Specified Attributes **49**

Partition a Rectangle Into Squares and Find the Total Number of Them **51**

Partition Shapes Into Equal Shares and Describe the Shares **53**

Individual Record Form **55**

Practice Test 1 . . . . **57**

Practice Test 2 . . . . **65**

Practice Test 3 . . . . **73**

About *Getting Ready for High-Stakes Assessment*

This *Getting Ready for High-Stakes Assessment* print guide consists of standards-based practice and practice tests.

Standards-Based Practice

The items in each practice set are designed to give students exposure to the wide variety of ways in which a standard may be assessed.

All standards-based practice sets are available to students online. Online item types include traditional multiple choice as well as technology-enhanced item types. The online practice experience also offers students hints, corrective feedback, and opportunities to try an item multiple times. You can assign online standards-based practice and receive instant access to student data and reports. The reports can help you pinpoint student strengths and weaknesses and tailor instruction to meet their needs. The standards-based practice sets in this guide mirror those found online; however, some technology-enhanced item types have been modified or replaced with items suitable for paper-and-pencil testing.

Practice Tests

Into Math also includes three practice tests designed to simulate high-stakes testing experiences similar to ones that students will encounter in the upper elementary grades. The practice tests are available online. Online item types include traditional multiple choice as well as technology-enhanced item types. You can assign the online tests for instant access to data and standards alignments. The practice tests in this guide mirror those found online; however, some technology-enhanced item types were modified or replaced with items suitable for paper-and-pencil testing. This guide includes record forms for these tests that show the content focus and depth of knowledge for each item.

Assessment Item Types

The high-stakes assessments students will take in the upper elementary grades contain item types beyond the traditional multiple-choice format. This allows for a more robust assessment of students' understanding of concepts and skills. High-stakes assessments are administered via computers, and *Into Math* presents items in formats similar to what students will see on the real tests. The following information is provided to help you familiarize your students with these different types of items. An example of each item type appears on the following pages. You may want to use the examples to introduce the item types to students. These pages describe the most common item types. You may find other types on some tests.

Example 1: Multiselect

Upon first glance, many students may easily confuse this item type with a traditional multiple-choice item. Explain to students that this type of item will have a special direction line that asks them to choose all the answers to the problem that are correct.

Which numbers are less than 25?

Choose the **2** correct answers.

○ 32   ○ 52

○ 24   ○ 17

Example 2: Fill in the Blank

Sometimes when students take a digital test, they will have to select a word, number, or symbol from a drop-down list or drag answer options into blanks. The print versions of the *Into Math* tests ask students to write the correct answer in the blank.

Ali puts 5 books in his bag. He puts 7 more books in his bag. How can Ali find the number of books in his bag?

Fill in the blanks with the correct numbers from the list to create an equation Ali could use.

_____ _____ _____

- - - - - - + - - - - - = - - - - - -

_____ _____ _____

| 2 | 5 | 7 | 12 |

Example 3: Classification

Some *Into Math* assessment items require students to categorize numbers or shapes. Digital versions of this item type require students to drag answer options into the correct place in a table. When the classification involves more complex equations or drawings, each object will have a letter next to it. Print versions of this item type will ask students to write answer options in the correct place in the table. Tell students that sometimes they may write the same number or word in more than one column of the table.

Write the numbers in the correct place in the table to show if they are greater than 31 or less than 31.

Greater than 31	Less than 31

47   33   29   89

Example 4: Matching

In some items, students will need to match one set of objects to another. In some computer-based items, students will need to drag an answer option into a box next to the element it matches. On paper-based tests, they do this by drawing a line connecting the two elements that match.

Draw a line to match each model with an equation. You will not use all the equations.

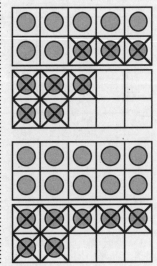

$$15 - 8 = 7$$

$$12 - 3 = 9$$

$$17 - 7 = 10$$

Example 5: Hotspot

Students may need to answer questions by interacting with a piece of art. On the digital tests, certain regions of the art are designated as "hot," meaning that students are able to click on them. Students click on the correct region or regions of the art to answer the question. On paper-based tests, students circle the correct region or regions of the art to answer the question.

Circle the **2** groups of coins that show 15 cents.

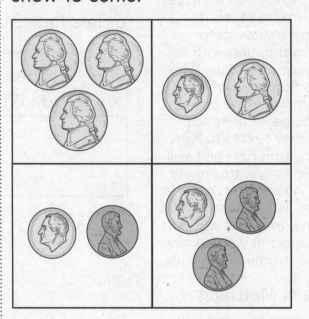

Example 6: Shading

Shading items allow students to select boxes to shade portions of an interactive rectangular array. In the print versions of these items, students shade a model to show the relationship being assessed.

Shade a fourth of the model.

1 Jerry picked 16 red apples. He picked 27 green apples. How many apples did Jerry pick?

Fill in the parts of the bar model and the blanks with the correct numbers.

_____ **apples**

_____

2 Brittany jumped rope for 18 minutes on Friday. She jumped rope for 48 minutes on Saturday. Which equation and answer show the number of minutes Brittany jumped rope?

○ ▢ = 48 − 18
  30 minutes

○ ▢ = 48 + 18
  56 minutes

○ ▢ = 48 + 18
  66 minutes

3 Ben has 37 pennies. Rachel has 22 more pennies than Ben. How many pennies does Rachel have?

_____ pennies

4 Kent's book has 64 pages. Kent reads 27 pages in the morning. He reads 18 pages that night. Use this model to show how many pages Kent needs to read to finish the book.

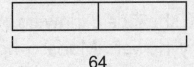

64

5 Logan counted 39 tadpoles in the pond. Eve counted 17 tadpoles. Which equation and answer show how many more tadpoles Logan counted than Eve counted?

○ $39 - \boxed{} = 17$

12 tadpoles

○ $17 + \boxed{} = 39$

22 tadpoles

○ $39 + 17 = \boxed{}$

56 tadpoles

6 John has 16 erasers. He gives 7 erasers to his cousin. Write an equation that shows how many erasers John has left.

_____

7 Alex has 67 stickers. He has 28 star stickers. The rest are animal stickers. Which equation and answer show how many animal stickers Alex has?

○ $67 + 28 = \boxed{}$

95 animal stickers

○ $28 + \boxed{} = 67$

41 animal stickers

○ $67 - 28 = \boxed{}$

39 animal stickers

8 Amy found 36 oak leaves. She found 41 maple leaves. How many leaves did Amy find?

_____ leaves

9 Marissa had some flowers. She gave 9 flowers to her mother. Now she has 8 flowers. Which equation and answer show how many flowers Marissa had to start?

○ $8 + \boxed{} = 9$ 1 flower

○ $\boxed{} - 9 = 8$ 17 flowers

○ $8 + 9 = \boxed{}$ 18 flowers

1 Which of these show a way to use doubles to add 4 + 5?

Choose the **2** correct answers.

○ 4 + 4 − 1

○ 4 + 4 + 1

○ 5 + 5 − 1

○ 5 + 5 + 1

2 Which of these shows a way to find 15 − 8?

○ 15 − 5 = 10 and
   10 − 4 = 6

○ 15 − 5 = 10 and
   10 − 3 = 7

○ 15 − 5 = 10 and
   10 − 2 = 8

3 Fill in the blanks with the correct numbers.

_____ + 5 = 13

13 + _____ = 18

20 − _____ = 13

4 What number is 15 more than 4 and 1 less than 20?

_____

5 Which shows how to count back to find 17 − 3?

○ 17, 16, 15

○ 17, 16, 15, 14

○ 17, 18, 19, 20

6 Fill in the blanks with the correct numbers.

$11 - 3 =$ _____

$11 - 4 =$ _____

$11 - 5 =$ _____

7. Which shows how to use a tens fact to subtract $12 - 8$?

○ $10 - 8 = 2$

○ $10 - 6 = 4$

○ $10 - 5 = 7$

8 Which of these shows a way to find $9 + 3$?

○ 9, 10, 11

○ 9, 8, 7, 6

○ 9, 10, 11, 12

9 Which of these equals 14? Choose the **2** correct answers.

○ $17 - 5$

○ $11 + 3$

○ $19 - 5$

○ $17 - 4$

10 Which of these show a way to add $9 + 7$?

Choose the **2** correct answers.

○ $7 + 3 + 6$

○ $7 + 4 + 6$

○ $9 + 1 + 6$

○ $9 + 2 + 6$

1 Mark has three walls with pictures.

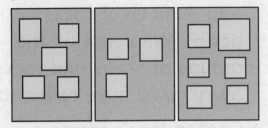

How many of Mark's walls have an even number of pictures?

○ 1

○ 2

○ 3

2 Jada buys three packages of barrettes.

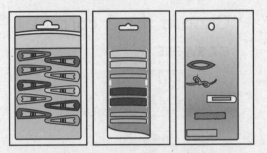

How many of Jada's packages have an odd number of barrettes?

○ 1

○ 2

○ 3

3 Which equation has a total that is odd?

○ 4 + 4 = ☐   ○ 7 + 7 = ☐   ○ 8 + 5 = ☐

4 Draw lines from the groups of flowers to **Even** or **Odd** to show if they have an even or odd number of flowers. You will use all the groups of flowers.

Even   **Odd**

5 Which pictures show an even number of balls?

Choose the **2** correct answers.

○

○

○

○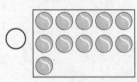

6 Ted has an even number of yellow markers and an odd number of green markers. What are all the groups of markers that could belong to Ted?

Choose the **2** correct answers.

○ 8 yellow markers and 3 green markers

○ 3 yellow markers and 5 green markers

○ 4 yellow markers and 2 green markers

○ 6 yellow markers and 7 green markers

7 Mary collects an odd number of shells and an odd number of rocks on the beach. What are all the groups of shells and rocks Mary could have collected?

Choose the **2** correct answers.

○ 9 shells and 6 rocks

○ 8 shells and 3 rocks

○ 5 shells and 7 rocks

○ 3 shells and 15 rocks

8 Which pictures show an odd number of marbles?

Choose the **2** correct answers.

○

○

○

○

1 Which equation shows how to find the total number of triangles?

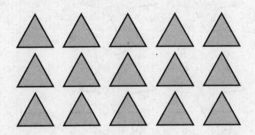

○ $5 + 3 = 8$

○ $5 + 5 = 10$

○ $5 + 5 + 5 = 15$

2 Which equation shows how to find the total number of letters?

○ $2 + 2 + 2 + 2 = 8$

○ $2 + 4 = 6$

○ $2 + 2 = 4$

3 David put his awards in 2 rows. He put 5 awards in each row. What is the total number of awards David puts in rows?

_____ awards

4 How many circles are there?

$3 + 3 + 3 + 3 =$ _____

5 Which equations show how to find the total number of flowers?

Choose the **2** correct answers.

○ $4 + 3 = 7$

○ $4 + 4 + 4 = 12$

○ $3 + 3 + 4 + 4 = 14$

○ $3 + 3 + 3 + 3 = 12$

6 How many squares are there?

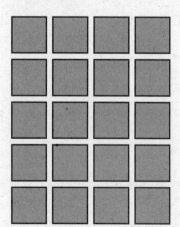

There are _____ squares.

7 How many stars are there?

$3 + 3 =$ _____

8 Lily plants her vegetables in 5 rows. Each row has 5 vegetables planted. How many vegetables did Lily plant?

_____ vegetables

1 Sonya has 140 beads. How many more bags of 10 beads does she need so that she will have 200 beads in all?

_____ bags of ten beads

2 How many groups of ten are in 300?

_____ groups of ten

3 Marcus is putting 10 packs of sticky notes in each of his boxes. How many packs of sticky notes will Marcus put in 20 boxes?

_____ packs of sticky notes

4 Markers come in boxes of 10. Ms. Nelson bought 800 markers for her school. How many boxes of markers did she buy?

_____ boxes

5 What does this model show?

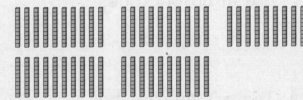

○ 5 tens
○ 5 hundreds
○ 50 hundreds

6 Mr. Grey has 20 packs of collectible cards. Each pack has 10 cards. He needs 700 cards for his store. How many more packs does Mr. Grey need?

_____ more packs

7 What number correctly completes the sentence?

There are _____ groups of ten in 400.

8 Napkins come in packages of 10. How many napkins are in 60 packages?

_____ napkins

9 The art teacher has 270 craft sticks. The craft sticks come in packs of 10. How many more packs are needed if the art teacher wants a total of 300 craft sticks?

_____ packs of ten

10 A grocery store has 90 packs of crackers. There are 10 crackers in each pack. How many crackers does the grocery store have?

_____ crackers

11 Which number has 5 hundreds?

○ 151
○ 355
○ 512

12 What number does this model show?

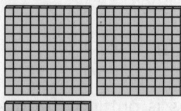
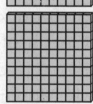

○ 30
○ 100
○ 300

1 Andrew fills jars with pennies. He has 5 jars with 100 pennies in each. How many pennies does Andrew have?

_____ pennies

2 What does this model show?
Choose the **3** correct answers.

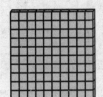

○ 10 tens
○ 100 ones
○ 1 hundred
○ 100 hundreds

3 How many hundreds are in 900?

_____ hundreds

4 Write how many tens. Write how many hundreds.
Write the number.

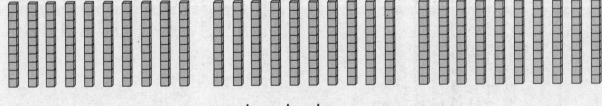

_____ tens   _____ hundreds   _____

5 How many hundreds are in 400?

_____ hundreds

6 Dog treats come in boxes of 100. Daniel bought 8 boxes. How many dog treats did Daniel buy?

_____ dog treats

7 What does this model show?

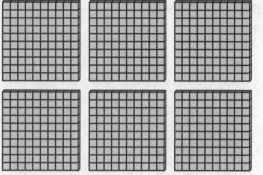

Choose the **2** correct answers.

○ 6 tens
○ 600 ones
○ 6 hundreds
○ 60 hundreds

8 Ms. Lee has 700 cans of food for the food bank. She will place 100 cans on each shelf.

How many shelves will she need?

_____ shelves

9 Write how many tens. Write how many hundreds. Write the number.

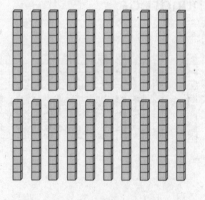

_____ tens   _____ hundreds   _____

10 Ahmed has 2 boxes of straws. Each box has 100 straws. He needs 800 straws. How many more boxes of straws does he need?

_____ more boxes

1 Jen starts at 280 and counts by tens.
What are the next 3 numbers Jen will say?

280, 290, _____, _____, _____

2 Skip-count by 5s.

35, _____, _____, _____

3 Choose the ways that show counting by tens.
Choose the **2** correct answers.

○ 550, 560, 570, 580, 590

○ 210, 310, 410, 510, 610

○ 650, 651, 652, 653, 654

○ 170, 180, 190, 200, 210

4 Jeff starts at 190 and counts by hundreds.
What are the next 3 numbers Jeff will say?

190, _____, _____, _____

Name _____

5 What number is missing from each pattern?

25, _____, 35, 40, 45

10, 20, 30, _____, 50

50, 60, 70, 80, _____

70, 75, _____, 85, 90

6 Which of these shows counting by fives?

○ 576, 577, 578, 579, 580

○ 120, 130, 140, 150, 160

○ 370, 375, 380, 385, 390

7 Some children are practicing counting. Which child will say more numbers?

○ Elsie counts by tens to 50.

○ Frank counts by fives to 20.

○ Jack counts by hundreds to 300.

8 Skip-count by hundreds.

300, _____, _____, _____

9 Tom counts by ones to 100. Jill counts by fives to 100. Rick counts by tens to 100. Which of these numbers will each of them say when they count?

○ 50

○ 51

○ 55

10 Which group of numbers shows counting by hundreds?

○ 500, 510, 520, 530

○ 700, 701, 702, 703

○ 600, 700, 800, 900

1 What is the value of the underlined digit?

15<u>3</u>

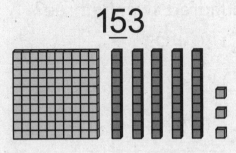

_____

2 What number do the words eight hundred five name?

_____

3 What are some ways to tell what the number 52 means?

Choose the **2** correct answers.

○ 52 ones

○ 52 tens

○ 50 tens and 2 ones

○ 5 tens and 2 ones

4 Patti sold 248 pencils. How can the meaning of this number be shown?

Choose the **2** correct ways.

○ 2 + 8 + 4

○ 20 + 40 + 8

○ 200 + 48

○ 200 + 40 + 8

5 Sally needs 300 stickers. Vince gives her 20 packs with 10 stickers in each pack. How many more stickers does Sally need?

_____ stickers

Name _____

6 Straws are sold in boxes, in bags, or as single straws. Each box has 10 bags in it. Each bag has 10 straws in it. Mr. Tan needs 355 straws. What are all the ways Mr. Tan can buy 355 straws?

Choose the **2** correct answers.

○ 3 bags and 55 straws

○ 35 bags and 5 straws

○ 3 boxes, 50 bags, and 5 straws

○ 3 boxes, 5 bags, and 5 straws

7 It is 154 days until Jeff's birthday. How can the number of days be written using expanded form?

_____ + _____ + 4 = 154

8 Terry has one hundred sixty-four marbles. How many marbles does Terry have?

_____ marbles

9 Which shows how to write the expanded form of four hundred twenty-three?

○ 40 + 23

○ 4 + 2 + 3

○ 400 + 20 + 3

10 What does this model show?

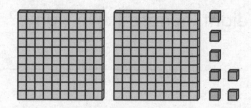

○ twenty-seven

○ two hundred seven

○ two hundred seventy

1 Which number sentence is true?

Choose the **2** correct answers.

○ 275 > 164

○ 424 > 417

○ 560 = 506

○ 823 < 710

2 Which number sentence is true?

Choose the **2** correct answers.

○ 209 > 641

○ 373 < 368

○ 465 = 465

○ 861 > 761

3 Which number sentence is true?

Choose the **2** correct answers.

○ 424 > 318

○ 108 > 150

○ 765 = 756

○ 850 < 984

4 Write the symbol that correctly compares the numbers. Write >, <, or =.

787 _____ 769

405 _____ 399

396 _____ 402

128 _____ 131

5 Write the symbol that correctly compares the numbers. Write >, <, or =.

343 _____ 328

705 _____ 699

691 _____ 706

115 _____ 120

Name _____

6 Write the symbol that correctly compares the numbers. Write >, <, or =.

183 _____ 138

182 _____ 208

947 _____ 947

428 _____ 392

---

7 Jill and Ed collect postcards. Jill has 124 postcards. Ed has 131 postcards.

Jill gets 10 more postcards. Ed gets 5 more postcards.

Who has more postcards now?

_____ has more postcards now.

---

8 Dan and Hannah collect toy cars. Dan has 132 cars. Hannah has 138 cars.

Dan gets 10 more cars. Hannah gets 3 more cars.

Who has more cars now?

_____ has more cars now.

9 Samantha and Brian collect trading cards. Samantha has 309 trading cards. Brian has 312 trading cards.

Samantha gets 10 more trading cards. Brian gets 6 more trading cards.

Who has more trading cards now?

_____ has more trading cards now.

---

10 Write the symbol that correctly compares the numbers. Write >, <, or =.

183 _____ 138

182 _____ 208

947 _____ 947

© Houghton Mifflin Harcourt Publishing Company

1 Which sums are equal to 76?

Choose the **2** correct answers.

○ 35 + 31
○ 49 + 27
○ 54 + 22
○ 68 + 18

2 Subtract 18 from 35. Which is a correct way to model 35 to be able to subtract 18?

○ 2 tens and 15 ones
○ 2 tens and 15 tens
○ 3 tens and 15 ones

3 Use the number line. Count up to find the difference.

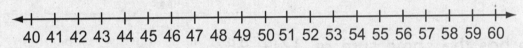

40 41 42 43 44 45 46 47 48 49 50 51 52 53 54 55 56 57 58 59 60

53 − 46 = _____

4 George collected 36 oak leaves. He collected 41 maple leaves. Break apart the addends to show how many leaves George collected.

$$
\begin{array}{r}
36 \rightarrow \underline{\hspace{1em}} + 6 \\
+\ 41 \rightarrow \underline{40 + \underline{\hspace{1em}}} \\
\hline
70 + 7 = \underline{\hspace{1em}}
\end{array}
$$

5 What is the difference?

65 − 8 = _____

Name _____

6 What is the sum?

$$\begin{array}{r} 65 \\ + 25 \\ \hline \end{array}$$

$65 + 25 =$ _____

---

7 What is the difference?

$$\begin{array}{r} 84 \\ - 37 \\ \hline \end{array}$$

$84 - 37 =$ _____

---

8 Which has the same sum as $32 + 48$?

Choose the **2** correct answers.

○ $15 + 75$
○ $18 + 62$
○ $22 + 48$
○ $56 + 24$

---

9 What is the sum?

$$\begin{array}{r} 48 \\ + 52 \\ \hline \end{array}$$

○ 80
○ 90
○ 100

10 What is the difference?

$$\begin{array}{r} 77 \\ - 55 \\ \hline \end{array}$$

○ 12
○ 22
○ 32

1 What is the sum?

$$17$$
$$42$$
$$+\ 26$$

The sum is _____.

2 What is the sum?

$$17$$
$$4$$
$$33$$
$$+\ 29$$

The sum is _____.

3 What is the sum?

$$41$$
$$34$$
$$+\ 22$$

The sum is _____.

4 Use the hundred chart to solve.

$35 + 18 = \boxed{}$

Circle the sum on the chart.

31	32	33	34	35	36	37	38	39	40
41	42	43	44	45	46	47	48	49	50
51	52	53	54	55	56	57	58	59	60

5 On four days of the week, Madelyn practiced her violin 23 minutes, 32 minutes, 16 minutes, and 25 minutes. How many tens and ones are in the sum of the minutes?

○ 9 tens and 6 ones

○ 8 tens and 6 ones

○ 9 tens and 16 ones

6 Leah put 21 white marbles, 31 black marbles, and 7 blue marbles in a bag. Then her sister added 19 yellow marbles. How many marbles are in the bag?

There are _____ marbles in the bag.

7 Which sums equal 100?

Choose the **2** correct answers.

○ 21 + 20 + 23 + 26

○ 26 + 21 + 28 + 24

○ 18 + 35 + 25 + 22

○ 20 + 15 + 40 + 25

8 There are 21 pencils, 14 pencils, 30 pencils, and 28 pencils in bins around the classroom. How many pencils are in the bins?

There are _____ pencils in the bins.

9 Which sums equal 60 or greater?

Choose the **2** correct answers.

○ 15 + 12 + 15 + 15

○ 15 + 16 + 15 + 15

○ 14 + 15 + 15 + 14

○ 15 + 12 + 18 + 16

© Houghton Mifflin Harcourt Publishing Company

1 Sydney's class collected 223 cans for recycling. Ramon's class collected 132 cans. How many cans did the classes collect altogether?

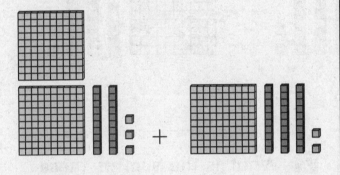

_____ cans

2 At the store, there are 463 rocks and shells. There are 42 rocks. How many shells are there at the store?

○ $\begin{array}{r} 463 \\ -\ 42 \\ \hline 43 \end{array}$

○ $\begin{array}{r} 463 \\ -\ 42 \\ \hline 421 \end{array}$

○ $\begin{array}{r} 463 \\ -\ 42 \\ \hline 442 \end{array}$

3 A birdwatcher counted 163 yellow birds and 185 brown birds.

$\begin{array}{r} 163 \rightarrow \quad 100+60+3 \\ +185 \rightarrow +100+80+5 \\ \hline \end{array}$

Which shows the number of birds the birdwatcher counted?

○ 2 hundreds 4 tens 8 ones

○ 3 hundreds 3 tens 7 ones

○ 3 hundreds 4 tens 8 ones

4 Add 231 and 248. How many hundreds, tens, and ones are in the sum?

_____ hundreds

_____ tens

_____ ones

Name _____

5 Add.

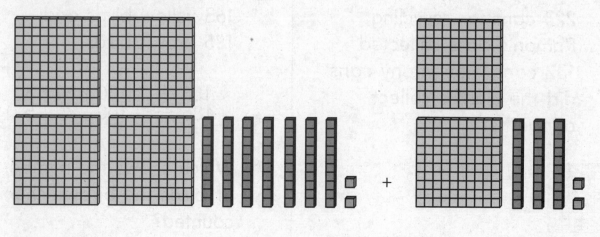

472 + 232 = _____

---

6 A store sells 154 DVDs and 88 CDs. How many more DVDs does the store sell than CDs?

Which sentences describe steps to solve the problem?

Choose the **2** correct answers.

○ Regroup 1 ten as 10 ones.

○ Subtract 8 tens from 14 tens.

○ Subtract 4 ones from 8 ones.

○ Regroup a hundred into 10 ones.

7 What is the sum of these numbers?

Hundreds	Tens	Ones
6	2	9
+ 2	5	6

○ 865   ○ 875   ○ 885

8 What is the difference of these numbers?

Hundreds	Tens	Ones
4	9	7
− 2	8	8

497 − 288 = _____

1 A store has 263 board games. It has 100 fewer puzzles than board games. The store has 10 more action figures than puzzles.

How many of each does the store have?

_____ board games

_____ puzzles

_____ action figures

2 Subtract.

659
− 10

What is the difference?

○ 559

○ 649

○ 669

3 Use the clues to answer the question.

• Shawn counts 213 cars.
• Maria counts 100 fewer cars than Shawn.
• Jayden counts 10 fewer than Maria.

How many cars does Jayden count?

_____ cars

4 Sanjo has 348 marbles. Harry has 100 more marbles than Sanjo. Abel has 10 more marbles than Harry.

Harry has _____ marbles.

Abel has _____ marbles.

5 Subtract.

721
−100

What is the difference?

○ 611

○ 621

○ 711

6 What is the sum?

$843 + 10 = ?$

○ 853

○ 943

○ 953

7 What is 100 more than 387?

100 more than 387 is _____.

8 Todd has 105 stickers. He gives 10 stickers to a friend. Then Todd buys 100 more stickers. How many stickers does Todd have now?

○ 95

○ 195

○ 215

9 What is 10 fewer than 309?

○ 300

○ 299

○ 289

10 Add.

$$\begin{array}{r} 446 \\ +100 \\ \hline \end{array}$$

The sum is _____.

1 Which sentences explain how to find the difference?

Tens	Ones
☐	☐
8	1
− 5	6

Choose the **2** correct answers.

○ Regroup a ten to make 11 ones.

○ Subtract 1 one from 6 ones.

○ Subtract 5 tens from 7 tens.

○ Subtract 5 tens from 8 tens.

2 Which shows a correct strategy to add 58 + 26?

○ 58 + 2 + 6

○ 58 + 10 + 6

○ 58 + 10 + 10 + 6

3 Which sentences explain how to find the difference?

Tens	Ones
☐	☐
6	2
− 2	5

Choose the **2** correct answers.

○ Subtract 2 ones from 5 ones.

○ Subtract 2 tens from 6 tens.

○ Regroup a ten to make 12 ones.

○ Subtract 5 ones from 12 ones.

4 Kylie is adding 46 + 32.

Which shows how Kylie correctly adds tens and ones?

○ 4 + 3 = 7
  60 + 20 = 80

○ 40 + 30 = 70
  6 + 2 = 8

○ 4 + 2 = 6
  60 + 30 = 90

5 Diana has 196 marbles. She gives away 42 of her marbles to her sister. What is one step Diana should follow to find how many marbles she has left?

- ◯ Subtract 6 ones from 12 ones.
- ◯ Subtract 2 ones from 6 ones.
- ◯ Ungroup 9 tens as 8 tens 10 ones.

6 Sean has 158 stickers. He gives away 39 stickers. What is one step Sean should follow to find how many stickers he has left?

- ◯ Subtract 8 ones from 9 ones.
- ◯ Regroup a ten to make 18 ones.
- ◯ Subtract 30 tens from 15 tens.

7 Which of these is one way to find 69 − 44?

- ◯ Subtract 6 − 4 and 9 − 4.
- ◯ Subtract 60 − 40 and 9 − 4.
- ◯ Subtract 60 − 40 and 90 − 40.

8 Which of these steps can be used to subtract 46 from 73?

Choose the **2** correct answers.

- ◯ Subtract 6 tens from 7 tens.
- ◯ Subtract 6 ones from 13 ones.
- ◯ Subtract 3 ones from 6 ones.
- ◯ Subtract 4 tens from 6 tens.

1 Owen wants to measure the length of a chalkboard in his classroom.

Which is the BEST choice of tool?

○ tiles

○ inch ruler

○ yardstick

2 Josh wants to measure the distance around a soccer ball. Which of these tools should Josh use?

○ measuring tape

○ yardstick

○ inch ruler

---

3 How long is this crayon to the nearest inch?

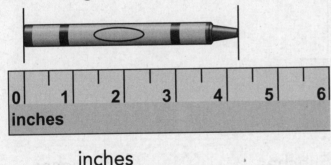

_____ inches

---

4 Susan uses unit cubes to measure the length of the yarn. Each unit cube is 1 centimeter long.

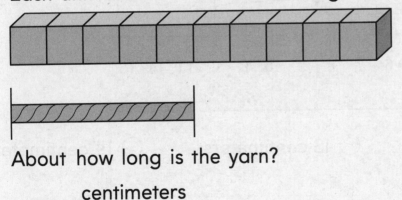

About how long is the yarn?

_____ centimeters

Name _____

5 About how many centimeters long is this rope?

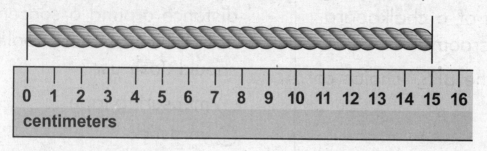

○ 12 centimeters   ○ 14 centimeters   ○ 15 centimeters

6 About how long is this leaf to the nearest inch?

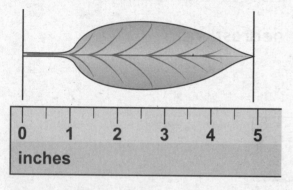

○ 4 inches   ○ 5 inches   ○ 10 inches

7 About how many centimeters long is this paintbrush?

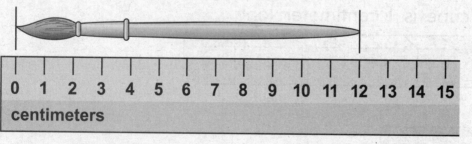

○ 12 centimeters   ○ 13 centimeters   ○ 14 centimeters

30

1 This toy boat is 5 little paper clips long.

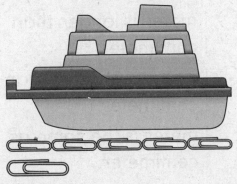

About how many big paper clips long is the toy boat?

The boat is about _____ big paper clips long.

The number of big paper clips is _____ because big paper clips are longer than the little paper clips.

2 Which of these is true about 1 foot?

○ 1 foot is the same as 1 inch.

○ 1 foot is shorter than 1 inch.

○ 1 foot is longer than 1 inch.

3 Sue measured her desk in centimeters. Then she measured it in meters. What will be true?

○ The number of centimeters is less than the number of meters.

○ The number of centimeters is greater than the number of meters.

○ The number of centimeters is the same as the number of meters.

4 Luis says a loaf of bread is 1 foot long.

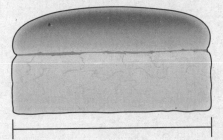

What will be true if Luis measures the bread in inches?

○ Inches are little, so there are more inches than feet.

○ Inches are little, so there are fewer inches than feet.

○ Inches and feet are both ways to measure, so they are the same.

Name _____

5 Pat measures his bedroom. It is more than 10 giant steps long. What will be true if he measures his bedroom in baby steps?

○ It will be about 10 baby steps long.

○ It will be less than 10 baby steps long.

○ It will be more than 10 baby steps long.

6 Mickey's teddy bear is 1 foot tall.

About how many inches tall is Mickey's teddy bear?

○ 1 inch

○ more than 1 inch

○ less than 1 inch

7 Which of these is true about 1 meter?

○ 1 meter is longer than 1 centimeter.

○ 1 meter is shorter than 1 centimeter.

○ 1 meter is the same as 1 centimeter.

8 A school room door is about 2 meters tall.

?

How many centimeters tall would the door be?

○ 2 centimeters

○ less than 2 centimeters

○ more than 2 centimeters

1 Ella lays 1-inch tiles in a line until the line has the same length as a football used in the high school football games.

Which sentence BEST estimates the length of the football?

○ A football is about 12 tiles long.

○ A football is less than 6 tiles long.

○ A football is more than 50 tiles long.

---

2 The paintbrush is about 7 centimeters long.

Which student has the BEST estimate?

○ Gavin says the feather is about 8 centimeters long.

○ Ray says the feather is about 5 centimeters long.

○ Justin says the feather is about 7 meters long.

---

3 The paper clip is about 4 centimeters long.

Which student has the BEST estimate for the length of the string?

○ Gale says the string is about 20 centimeters long.

○ Robin says the string is about 10 centimeters long.

○ Beth says the string is about 5 centimeters long.

---

4 Write meters or centimeters for the BEST estimate of length.

A driveway is 8 _____ long.

A couch is 2 _____ long.

A pen is 15 _____ long.

5 Write feet or inches for the BEST estimate of length.

A teacher is 65 _____ tall.

A bus is 48 _____ long.

The curtains are 80 _____ long.

6 Write meters or centimeters for the BEST estimate of length.

A juice box is 10 _____ tall.

A TV is 100 _____ wide.

A bookcase is 2 _____ tall.

---

7 Use the 1-inch mark. Estimate the length of each piece of string.

The top string is about

_____ inches long.

The bottom string is

about _____ inches long.

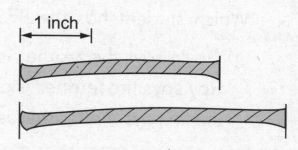

---

8 Luna bought a new rug for her bedroom. Which is the BEST estimate for the length of her rug?

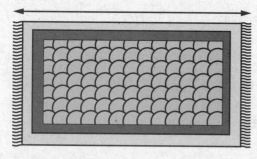

○ 2 feet

○ 12 inches

○ 12 feet

1 A piece of yarn and a crayon
are measured. Which sentences
are true?

Choose the **2** correct answers.

○ The yarn is 12 centimeters long.

○ The yarn is 3 centimeters longer than the crayon.

○ The crayon is 8 centimeters long.

○ The crayon is 11 centimeters shorter than the yarn.

2 The lengths of 2 pencils are measured.

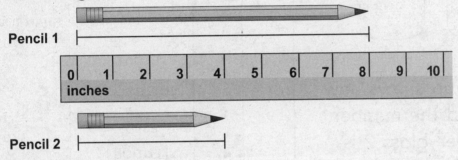

Which sentence is true?

○ Pencil 1 is 4 inches longer than pencil 2.

○ Pencil 1 is 6 inches longer than pencil 2.

○ Pencil 2 is 4 inches longer than pencil 1.

3 A paper clip and a paintbrush
are measured in centimeters.

How much longer is the
paintbrush than the paper clip?

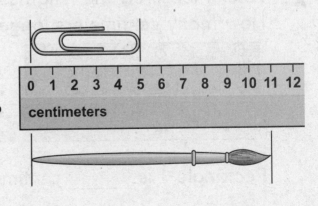

○ 5 centimeters longer

○ 6 centimeters longer

○ 7 centimeters longer

Name _____

4 Holly measures 2 glasses.

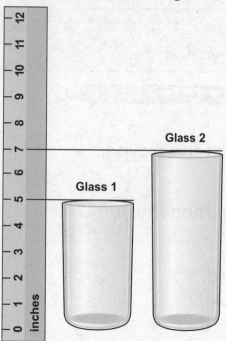

Which equation shows how Holly can find the number of inches taller glass 2 is than glass 1?

○ 7 − 6 = 1
○ 7 − 5 = 2
○ 7 − 4 = 3

5 How much taller is the bottle of shampoo than the bottle of lotion?

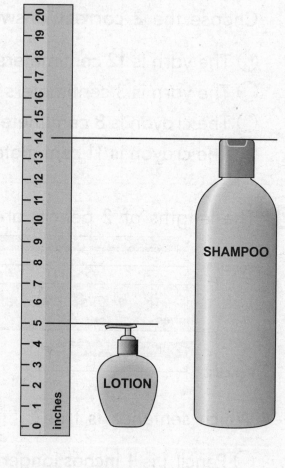

_____ inches

6 Peter measured the lengths of 2 rectangles in centimeters. How many centimeters longer is rectangle 1 than rectangle 2?

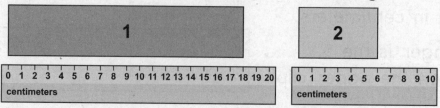

Rectangle 1 is _____ centimeters longer than rectangle 2.

1 Meg has a piece of material that is 9 centimeters long.
She has another piece of material that is 11 centimeters long.
How many centimeters of material does Meg have altogether?

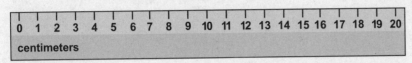

Meg has _____ centimeters of material.

---

2 Michael has 54 centimeters of brown yarn. He has 16 more
centimeters of yellow yarn than brown yarn.

Part A

What operation completes the equation to show how to find
how many centimeters of yellow yarn Michael has?

54 _____ 16 = ▢

Part B

How many centimeters of yellow yarn does Michael have?

Michael has _____ centimeters of yellow yarn.

---

3 A paper clip is 7 centimeters long. A fork is 18 centimeters
long. How much longer is the fork than the paper clip?

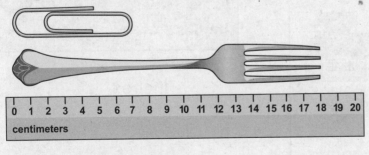

_____ centimeters

4 Carli measures 2 sticks. One stick is 16 inches long and the other stick is 22 inches long. How many inches long are both sticks combined?

○ 28

○ 30

○ 38

5 Jack measures 4 rocks. What is the combined length of Jack's rocks?

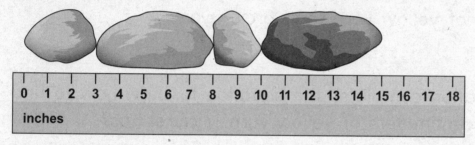

_____ inches

6 How much taller is the building than the house?

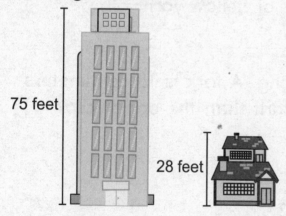

75 feet

28 feet

○ 47 feet

○ 50 feet

○ 53 feet

7 What is the difference between the lengths of the bracelets?

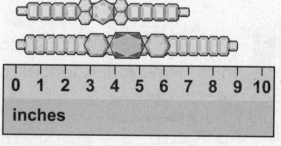

_____ inches

1 A poster board is 14 inches long. Seth cuts off 5 inches. How long is the poster board now?

Mark the number line to show the answer.

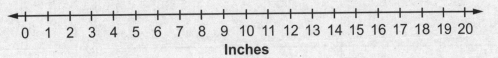

Inches

2 Pamela has a ribbon that is 35 centimeters long. She has another ribbon that is 8 centimeters long. How long are the 2 ribbons together?

Mark the number line to show the answer.

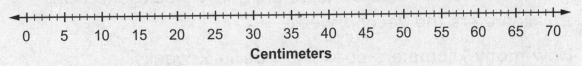

Centimeters

3 Mara had 4 meters of fabric. Her mom gave her 6 meters of fabric. Then she found another 5 meters of fabric. How many meters of fabric does Mara have now?

Mark the number line to show the answer.

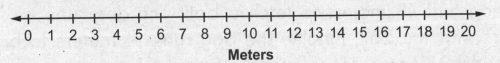

Meters

4 What subtraction problem is shown on the number line?

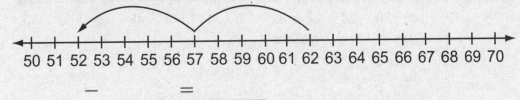

_____ − _____ = _____

5 Ryan has 18 centimeters of silver wire. He has another wire that is 9 centimeters long.

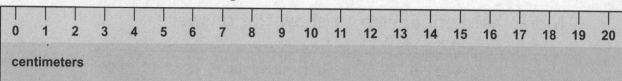

Ryan uses the ruler to find the difference in length between the 2 wires. What is the difference in length in centimeters?

_____ centimeters

---

6 Marisol rides her bike 34 kilometers in 1 week. She rides 27 kilometers the second week.

How many kilometers does she ride in 2 weeks?

Mark the number line to show the answer.

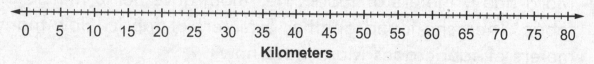

---

7 Steve's dog runs 19 meters to fetch a ball. The dog runs 23 meters with the ball. Finally, the dog runs 14 meters to bring the ball back to Steve. How far does Steve's dog run?

Mark the number line to show the answer.

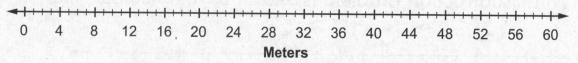

1 Jim looks at his clock. The hour hand is pointing between 11 and 12. The minute hand is pointing to the 5.

Which clock does Jim see?

○

○

○

2 What time is shown on this clock?

Choose the **2** correct answers.

○ 3:45 a.m.

○ 9:15 p.m.

○ half past 9

○ 15 minutes past nine

3 What time does this clock show?

_____ : _____

4 Which clock shows 15 minutes before 7:00?

5 What time is shown on this clock?

_____ : _____

6 What time does this clock show?

_____ : _____

7 John's soccer game began at 7:10 a.m. Which clock shows the time the soccer game began?

1 Antoine gave Fran these coins. How much money did Antoine give Fran?

_____ ¢

2 Jackie paid for a notebook with the money shown. The notebook cost exactly this amount. How much did the notebook cost?

_____ ¢

3 Which group of coins have a total value of 75 cents?

Choose the **3** correct answers.

○ 3 quarters

○ 1 quarter, 2 dimes, and 3 nickels

○ 6 dimes, 2 nickels, and 5 pennies

○ 10 nickels and 25 pennies

4 Jose wants to buy a bottle of juice for $0.74. Which shows the exact amount Jose needs to buy the bottle of juice?

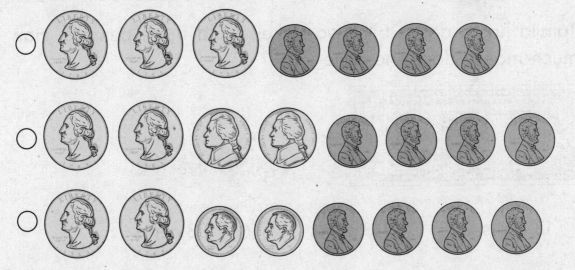

5 Which picture shows the number of quarters needed to make a dollar?

___

6 What is the value of a dime?

○ 25 cents   ○ 10 cents   ○ 5 cents

___

7 Jamila has a dollar bill, two nickels, and three pennies. How much money does she have in all?

○ 13 cents   ○ 113 cents   ○ 123 cents

1 Ali has measured the length of some leaves in centimeters. He has found that some leaves are 10 centimeters long. He found that some others are 12 or 13 centimeters long. Ali started to make a line plot to show the lengths. What numbers are missing from his line plot?

My Leaves

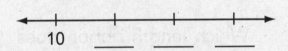

10 ___ ___ ___

**Length of Leaves
(in centimeters)**

2 Carol and her brother measure some ropes. They wrote the measurements on this chart.

**Lengths
of Ropes
(in meters)**

5	7
4	5
6	6

Which line plot shows the same measurements?

○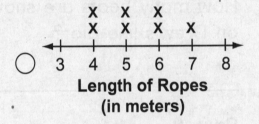

**Length of Ropes
(in meters)**

○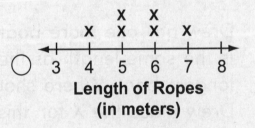

**Length of Ropes
(in meters)**

○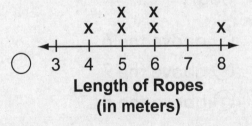

**Length of Ropes
(in meters)**

3 Use this information to answer Parts A and B.

Drew measured the lengths of his toy boats. Then he made this line plot.

Drew's Boats

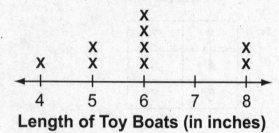

Length of Toy Boats (in inches)

Part A

How many boats are shown on Drew's line plot?

_____

Part B

Drew got one more boat. It is the same length as the longest boat. Where should Drew place the X for this boat?

○ above the 6

○ above the 7

○ above the 8

4 Use this information to answer Parts A and B.

Dora measured all of her ribbons. She made this line plot to show how many of each length she has.

Dora's Ribbons

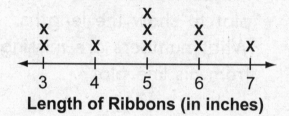

Length of Ribbons (in inches)

Part A

Which length ribbon does Dora have the most of?

○ 5 inches

○ 6 inches

○ 7 inches

Part B

Dora finds 2 ribbons that are each 6 inches long. She puts an X for each of them on her line plot. How many ribbons does her line plot show now?

_____

1 Mr. King is making a graph to show how many children rode the bus each day. He knows that 1 more student rode the bus on Wednesday than on Tuesday.

Children Who Rode the Bus						
Monday	🚌	🚌	🚌	🚌	🚌	
Tuesday	🚌	🚌				
Wednesday						
Thursday	🚌	🚌	🚌	🚌		

Key: Each  is 1 child.

Which picture shows how to finish the graph?

○ 🚌 🚌

○ 🚌 🚌 🚌

○ 🚌 🚌 🚌 🚌

2 The number of people that like green should be 2 more than the number of people that like red.

Shade the graph to show the correct number of people that like green.

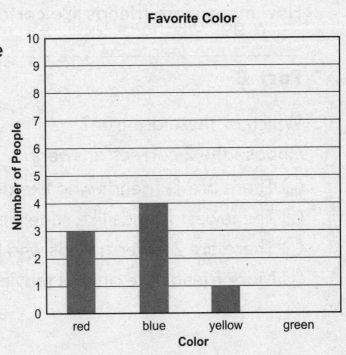

3 Kim made this graph to show her friends' favorite kinds of movies.

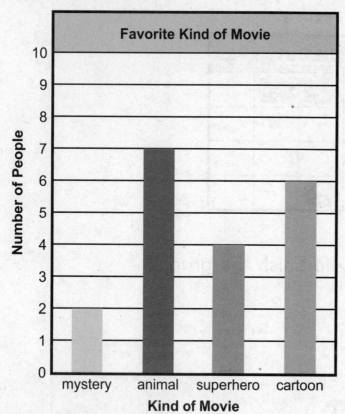

Part A

How many more friends like cartoons than mysteries?

_____

Part B

Which of these are true?

Choose the **2** correct answers.

○ There are 11 friends who like animal or superhero movies best.

○ The fewest friends like superhero movies best.

○ There are 2 fewer friends who like mysteries than like cartoons.

○ More friends like animal movies than mysteries.

1 Which of these is a
drawing of a cube?

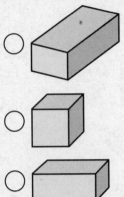

○

○

○

2 What can this shape be
called?

Choose the **2** correct
answers.

○ square
○ triangle
○ quadrilateral
○ pentagon

3 Which of these shapes is a
pentagon?

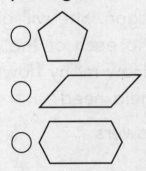

○

○

○

4 Clark draws a picture of
3 different quadrilaterals.
How many sides does he
draw?

○ 4
○ 6
○ 12

5 Compare a pentagon and a quadrilateral.

A pentagon has _____ sides.

It has _____ more side(s) than a quadrilateral.

6 Pamela is making a picture frame in the shape of a hexagon. She will glue a flower to each of the vertices. How many flowers does Pamela need?

_____ flowers

7 Which of these shapes is a hexagon?

○

○

○

8 Which of these shapes has 4 sides that can all be different lengths?

○ square
○ rectangle
○ quadrilateral

9 Which sentences are true about a cube?

Choose the **2** correct answers.

○ A cube 12 edges.
○ A cube has 16 edges.
○ A cube has 6 square faces.
○ A cube has only 4 square faces.

10 How many fewer vertices does a triangle have than a quadrilateral?

_____

1 Max is making a row of
equal-size squares inside
this rectangle.

How many more squares of
the same size does Max
need to make to finish the
row?

_____

2 How many equal-size small
squares are in this
rectangle?

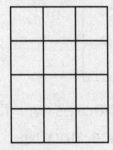

○ 9
○ 10
○ 12

---

3 These rectangles show rows and columns of equal-size squares.

Draw a line from the rectangle to the statement it matches.
You will not use all the statements.

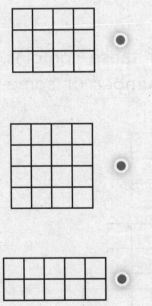

●   ● | 2 rows and 4 columns |

●   ● | 2 rows and 5 columns |

●   ● | 4 rows and 4 columns |

●   ● | 3 rows and 4 columns |

Name _____

4 Grace began drawing 2 rows of equal-size squares in this rectangle.

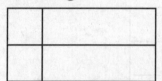

How many squares will there be when Grace finishes drawing the squares?

_____

5 Mary is drawing lines to make rows and columns of equal squares in this rectangle. How many more squares does Mary need to draw?

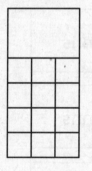

_____

6 Use this drawing to answer Parts A and B.

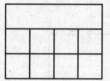

Part A

How many more same-size squares are needed to finish filling this rectangle?

_____ more squares

Part B

How many same-size squares will there be when it is finished?

_____ squares

7 Which of these contains the LEAST number of same-size squares?

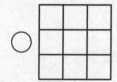

1 Which shows a half of the shape shaded?

2 Tyler cut a cookie into 4 equal pieces. He gave one of the pieces to his sister. How much of the cookie did Tyler give his sister?

○ a fourth

○ a third

○ a half

3 Which rectangles show a fourth shaded?

Choose the **2** correct answers.

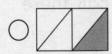

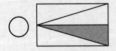

Name _____

4 Which shape shows a third shaded?

○

○

5 Which sentence BEST describes a shape that shows thirds?

○ The shape shows 3 shares.
○ The shape shows equal shares.
○ The shape shows 3 equal shares.

6 Martin cut an apple into 2 equal pieces. He ate 1 of the pieces. What part of the apple did Martin eat?

○ a half
○ a fourth
○ a quarter

7 Shade the model to show a fourth.

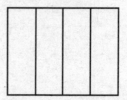

8 Shade the rectangle to show a half.

9 Shade the model to show 3 thirds.

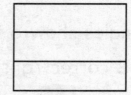

10 Callie cut a piece of paper into 4 equal parts. What should Callie call these pieces?

○ 4 thirds
○ 4 fourths
○ 4 halves

Practice Test

Item	Content Focus	DOK	Record
1	Fluently add and subtract within 20 using mental strategies.	1	
2	Use addition and subtraction within 100 to solve one- and two-step word problems.	2	
3	Fluently add and subtract within 20 using mental strategies.	2	
4	Add and subtract within 1000.	2	
5	Add and subtract within 1000.	1	
6	Add and subtract within 1000.	1	
7	Measure the length of an object to the nearest in., ft, cm, or m.	1	
8	Generate measurement data and show the data by making a line plot.	2	
9	Estimate lengths using units of in., ft, yd, cm, and m.	2	
10	Measure the length of an object to the nearest in., ft, cm, or m.	1	
11	Determine whether a group of objects (up to 20) has an odd or even number of members.	1	
12	Read and write numbers to 1000.	1	
13	Read and write numbers to 1000.	1	
14	Count within 1000; skip-count by 5s, 10s, and 100s.	1	
15	Recognize and draw shapes having specified attributes.	1	
16	Recognize and draw shapes having specified attributes.	1	
17	Recognize and draw shapes having specified attributes.	2	
18	Partition circles and rectangles into equal shares and describe the shares.	1	
19	Use addition and subtraction within 100 to solve one- and two-step word problems.	2	
20	Add up to four two-digit numbers.	1	
21	Add up to four two-digit numbers.	1	
22	Fluently add and subtract within 100.	1	
23	Draw a picture graph and a bar graph to represent a data set.	2	
24	Draw a picture graph and a bar graph to represent a data set.	2	
25	Use addition and subtraction within 100 to solve word problems involving lengths that are given in the same units.	2	

This page intentionally left blank.

1 Which shows a related addition fact?

$$15 - 8 = 7$$

○ $5 + 8 = 13$

○ $7 + 8 = 15$

○ $15 + 7 = 22$

2 There are 9 bugs on the grass and 5 bugs on a leaf. Which equation shows how many bugs there are in all?

○ $9 + 5 = 14$

○ $9 - 5 = 4$

○ $5 + 4 = 9$

3 Gina has 4 green toy trains, 2 red toy trains, and 6 yellow toy trains. How many toy trains does Gina have in all?

○ 6

○ 10

○ 12

4 There are 725 students in the school. There are 343 boys. How many girls are there?

Hundreds	Tens	Ones
▢	▢	▢
7	2	5
− 3	4	3

○ 382

○ 422

○ 482

5 What is the sum?

$$\begin{array}{r} 378 \\ +215 \\ \hline \end{array}$$

○ 583

○ 593

○ 693

6 What is the difference?

$$\begin{array}{r} 402 \\ -173 \\ \hline \end{array}$$

○ 339

○ 329

○ 229

---

7 What is the length of the ribbon to the nearest inch?

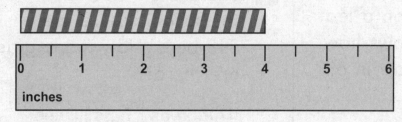

○ 9 inches

○ 8 inches

○ 4 inches

8 Use the line plot.

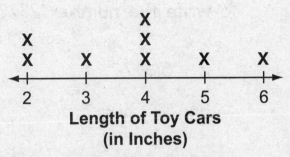

**Length of Toy Cars
(in Inches)**

How many toy cars are
3 inches long?

○ 1

○ 2

○ 4

9 Which is the BEST estimate
of the length of a baseball
bat?

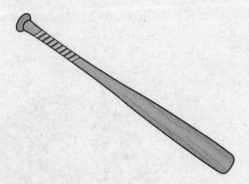

○ 2 feet

○ 8 feet

○ 10 feet

10 Francisco wants to measure
the distance around a ball.
Which is the BEST tool for
Francisco to use?

○ counters

○ measuring tape

○ pencil

11 Ms. Angeles writes an odd
number on the board.
Which could be the number
that Ms. Angeles writes?

○ 3

○ 6

○ 8

12 What is the value of the underlined digit?

<u>3</u>8

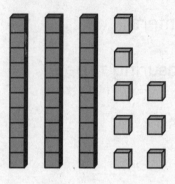

- ○ 3
- ○ 30
- ○ 80

13 Which shows another way to write the number 257?

- ○ 2 + 5 + 7
- ○ 200 + 7 + 5
- ○ 200 + 50 + 7

14 Which group of numbers shows counting by hundreds?

- ○ 300, 310, 320, 330
- ○ 500, 600, 700, 800
- ○ 600, 605, 610, 615

15 Which object has 2 circular surfaces?

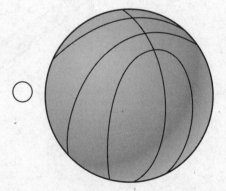

○   ○   ○

16 Which names a shape with
4 sides and 4 vertices?

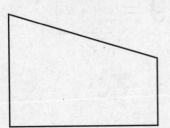

○ triangle

○ quadrilateral

○ pentagon

17 Which of these shapes has
FEWER than 4 angles?

○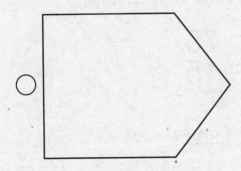

○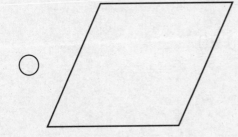

○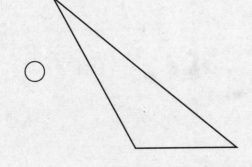

18 Which shows one half of
the shape shaded?

○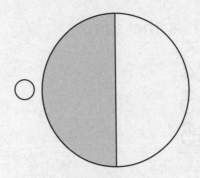

○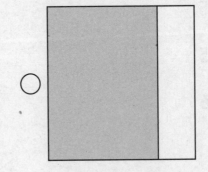

○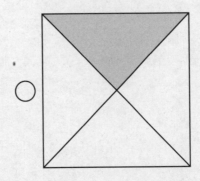

19 A store sold 21 green rings and 38 red rings. Which equation tells how many rings the store sold?

○ 12 + 38 = 50

○ 21 + 38 = 59

○ 38 − 21 = 17

20 What is the sum?

$$\begin{array}{r} 24 \\ 15 \\ +36 \\ \hline \end{array}$$

○ 65

○ 75

○ 76

21 What is the sum?

$$64 + 9 = \boxed{}$$

○ 63

○ 73

○ 75

22 What is the sum?

$$\begin{array}{r} 75 \\ +15 \\ \hline \end{array}$$

○ 80

○ 85

○ 90

23 Use the picture graph.

Favorite Color				
blue	☺	☺	☺		
green	☺	☺			
red	☺	☺	☺	☺	☺

Key: Each ☺ stands for 1 child.

How many children in all picked a favorite color?

○ 7　　　　　○ 10　　　　　○ 11

24 Use the picture graph.

Favorite Color				
blue	☺	☺	☺		
green	☺	☺			
red	☺	☺	☺	☺	☺

Key: Each ☺ stands for 1 child.

2 more children choose green. How many ☺ should be in the green row now?

○ 4　　　　　○ 5　　　　　○ 7

25 A crayon is 8 centimeters long. A spoon is 13 centimeters long. How much longer is the spoon than the crayon?

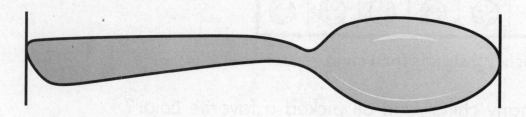

○ 3 centimeters

○ 5 centimeters

○ 21 centimeters

1 Which shows a related subtraction fact?

$$9 + 5 = 14$$

○ $19 - 14 = 5$

○ $14 - 5 = 9$

○ $9 - 5 = 4$

2 There were 16 birds at the park. Then 9 birds flew away. Which equation shows how many birds are at the park now?

○ $16 + 9 = 25$

○ $16 - 9 = 7$

○ $16 - 9 = 6$

3 Fran picks 3 red flowers, 7 yellow flowers, and 3 pink flowers. How many flowers does Fran pick in all?

○ 10

○ 12

○ 13

4 There are 429 students at the museum. There are 180 boys. How many girls are at the museum?

Hundreds	Tens	Ones
☐	☐	☐
4	2	9
− 1	8	0

○ 249

○ 349

○ 369

5 What is the sum?

$$
\begin{array}{r}
263 \\
+451 \\
\hline
\end{array}
$$

○ 714

○ 724

○ 614

6 What is the difference?

$$
\begin{array}{r}
507 \\
-368 \\
\hline
\end{array}
$$

○ 139

○ 149

○ 239

7 What is the length of the pencil to the nearest inch?

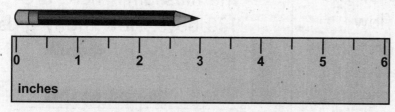

○ 3 inches

○ 6 inches

○ 7 inches

8 Use the line plot.

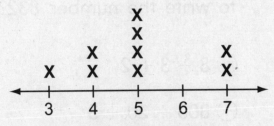

**Length of Toy Trucks
(in inches)**

How many toy trucks are
4 inches long?

○ 1

○ 2

○ 4

9 Which is the BEST estimate
of the length of a park
bench?

○ 1 foot

○ 6 feet

○ 15 feet

10 Frank wants to measure the
length of a bus.

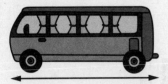

Which is the BEST tool for
Frank to use?

○ yardstick

○ counters

○ pencil

11 Ms. Ikeda writes an even
number on the board.
Which could be the number
that Ms. Ikeda writes?

○ 11

○ 13

○ 14

12 What is the value of the underlined digit?

4<u>5</u>

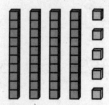

○ 4

○ 40

○ 50

13 Which shows another way to write the number 832?

○ 8 + 3 + 2

○ 800 + 20 + 3

○ 800 + 30 + 2

14 Which group of numbers shows counting by tens?

○ 100, 110, 120, 130

○ 200, 205, 210, 215

○ 300, 301, 302, 303

15 Which object has only 1 circular surface?

   ○

○

○
TUNA

16 Which names a shape with 6 sides and 6 vertices?

○ quadrilateral

○ pentagon

○ hexagon

17 Which of these shapes has FEWER than 5 angles?

○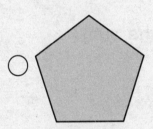

○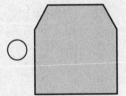

○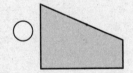

18 Which shows a third of the shape shaded?

○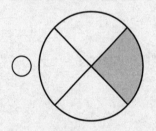

○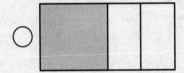

○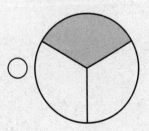

19 Beth has 26 stickers. Ken has 51 stickers. Which equation tells how many stickers Beth and Ken have in all?

○ $51 - 26 = 25$

○ $26 + 51 = 77$

○ $15 + 26 = 41$

20 What is the sum?

$$\begin{array}{r} 18 \\ 32 \\ +12 \\ \hline \end{array}$$

○ 52

○ 60

○ 62

21 What is the sum?

$$23 + 8 = \boxed{}$$

○ 21

○ 31

○ 32

22 What is the sum?

$$\begin{array}{r} 57 \\ +14 \\ \hline \end{array}$$

○ 61

○ 63

○ 71

23 Use the picture graph.

Favorite Muffin					
berry	😊	😊	😊		
corn	😊	😊	😊	😊	😊
pumpkin	😊				

Key: Each 😊 stands for 1 child.

How many children in all picked a favorite muffin?

○ 8   ○ 9   ○ 10

24 Use the picture graph.

Favorite Muffin					
berry	😊	😊	😊		
corn	😊	😊	😊	😊	😊
pumpkin	😊				

Key: Each 😊 stands for 1 child.

2 more children chose pumpkin. How many 😊 should be in the pumpkin row now?

○ 3   ○ 4   ○ 5

25 A rope is 10 centimeters long. A paintbrush is 12 centimeters long. How much longer is the paintbrush than the rope?

○ 1 centimeter

○ 2 centimeters

○ 22 centimeters

1 Which shows a related addition fact?

$17 - 9 = 8$

○ $17 + 9 = 26$

○ $9 + 7 = 16$

○ $8 + 9 = 17$

2 There are 7 big dogs and 6 small dogs. Which equation shows how many dogs there are in all?

○ $7 + 6 = 13$

○ $7 - 1 = 6$

○ $10 + 7 = 17$

3 Tess collects 2 green leaves, 8 red leaves, and 5 yellow leaves. How many leaves does Tess collect in all?

○ 10

○ 13

○ 15

4 There are 545 seats in the theater. 362 seats are filled. How many seats are empty?

Hundreds	Tens	Ones
▢	▢	▢
5	4	5
− 3	6	2

○ 283

○ 223

○ 183

5 What is the sum?

$$\begin{array}{r} 179 \\ +515 \\ \hline \end{array}$$

○ 794

○ 694

○ 684

6 What is the difference?

$$\begin{array}{r} 803 \\ -427 \\ \hline \end{array}$$

○ 476

○ 386

○ 376

7 What is the length of the paintbrush to the nearest inch?

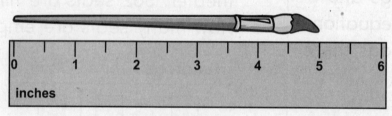

○ 5 inches

○ 10 inches

○ 11 inches

8 Use the line plot.

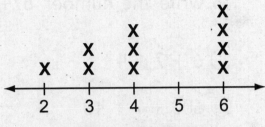

Length of Toy Planes (in inches)

How many toy planes are 4 inches long?

○ 2

○ 3

○ 4

9 Which is the BEST estimate of the length of a grownup's shoe?

○ 1 foot

○ 3 feet

○ 5 feet

10 Eddie wants to measure the distance around a water bottle.

Which is the BEST tool for Eddie to use?

○ counters

○ pencil

○ measuring tape

11 Ms. Martinez writes an even number on the board. Which could be the number that Ms. Martinez writes?

○ 11

○ 10

○ 9

12 What is the value of the underlined digit?

6̲2

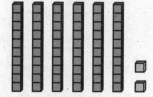

- ○ 6
- ○ 20
- ○ 60

13 Which shows another way to write the number 674?

- ○ 6 + 7 + 4
- ○ 600 + 7 + 40
- ○ 600 + 70 + 4

14 Which group of numbers shows counting by fives?

- ○ 400, 405, 410, 415
- ○ 500, 510, 520, 530
- ○ 600, 700, 800, 900

15 Which object has MORE than 2 flat surfaces?

 ○ 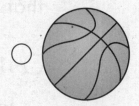 ○  ○

16 Which names a shape with 5 sides and 5 vertices?

○ quadrilateral

○ pentagon

○ hexagon

---

17 Which of these shapes has MORE than 5 sides?

○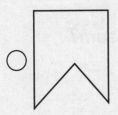

○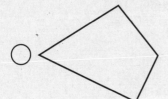

○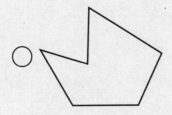

18 Which shows a fourth of the shape shaded?

○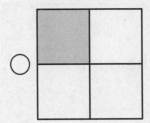

○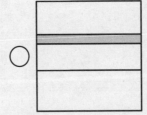

○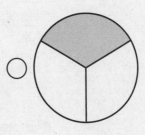

19 Jen has 52 beads. She buys 17 more beads. Which equation tells how many beads Jen has now?

○ 52 + 17 = 69

○ 52 − 17 = 35

○ 25 + 17 = 42

21 What is the sum?

$$47 + 6 = \boxed{}$$

○ 43

○ 52

○ 53

20 What is the sum?

$$\begin{array}{r} 43 \\ 27 \\ +13 \\ \hline \end{array}$$

○ 73

○ 80

○ 83

22 What is the sum?

$$\begin{array}{r} 38 \\ +23 \\ \hline \end{array}$$

○ 51

○ 55

○ 61

23 Use the picture graph.

Favorite Meal					
breakfast	🙂	🙂			
lunch	🙂	🙂	🙂		
dinner	🙂	🙂	🙂	🙂	🙂

Key: Each 🙂 stands for 1 child.

How many children picked a favorite meal?

○ 9   ○ 10   ○ 11

24 Use the picture graph.

Favorite Meal					
breakfast	🙂	🙂			
lunch	🙂	🙂	🙂		
dinner	🙂	🙂	🙂	🙂	🙂

Key: Each 🙂 stands for 1 child.

2 more children choose lunch. How many 🙂 should be in the lunch row now?

○ 4   ○ 5   ○ 7

25 A string is 9 centimeters long. A paper clip is 5 centimeters long. How much longer is the string than the paper clip?

○ 4 centimeters

○ 5 centimeters

○ 14 centimeters